ROCKS AND MINERALS

SEDIMENTARY ROCKS

by Rebecca E. Hirsch

Content Consultant
Dr. Kevin Theissen
Associate Professor and Chair
Department of Geology
University of Saint Thomas

Core Library

An Imprint of Abdo Publishing
www.abdopublishing.com

www.abdopublishing.com

Published by Abdo Publishing, a division of ABDO, PO Box 398166,
Minneapolis, Minnesota 55439. Copyright © 2015 by Abdo Consulting
Group, Inc. International copyrights reserved in all countries. No part of
this book may be reproduced in any form without written permission from
the publisher. Core Library™ is a trademark and logo of Abdo Publishing.

Printed in the United States of America, North Mankato, Minnesota
042014
092014

Cover Photo: Chris Gardiner/Thinkstock
Interior Photos: Chris Gardiner/Thinkstock, 1; Keantian/Shutterstock
Images, 4; Kojihirano/Thinkstock, 7; Stanislav Fosenbauer/Shutterstock
Images, 9, 45; Shutterstock Images, 10, 32; Neil A Rodrigues/Shutterstock
Images, 12; Sílvia Antunes/Thinkstock, 15, 16 (top middle); Moodboard/
Thinkstock, 16 (top left); Bunyos/Thinkstock, 16 (top right); Anneleven/
Thinkstock, 16 (bottom left); Juergen Faelchle/Shutterstock Images, 16
(bottom middle); Liveshot/Shutterstock Images, 16 (bottom right); Sumit
Buranarothtrakul/Thinkstock, 18; Bambuh/Shutterstock Images, 21;
Thinkstock, 24, 42 (top); Dkaranouh/Thinkstock, 28; National Park Service,
30, 43; Porojnicu/Thinkstock, 35; Marcel Clemens/Shutterstock Images, 37;
Red Line Editorial, 40; Jacek Sopotnicki/Thinkstock, 42 (bottom)

Editor: Jenna Gleisner
Series Designer: Becky Daum

Library of Congress Control Number: 2014932344

Cataloging-in-Publication Data
Hirsch, E. Rebecca.
 Sedimentary rocks / Rebecca E. Hirsch.
  p. cm. -- (Rocks and minerals)
Includes bibliographical references and index.
ISBN 978-1-62403-390-2
1. Sedimentary rocks1--Juvenile literature.   I. Title.
552/.5--dc23

2014932344

CONTENTS

CHAPTER ONE

WHAT ARE SEDIMENTARY ROCKS?

After a heavy rain, muddy puddles often form on the ground. Stream, river, or lake water turns brown. What causes the water to turn a muddy color? The color is caused by sediment—tiny particles of dirt and rocks that float in the water. During a heavy rainfall, rain washes away bits of rock from the ground. The bits are washed downstream.

Erosion of sediment causes rivers or lakes to look muddy.

This is called erosion. Over time, the sediment settles to the bottom. The water becomes clear again.

The Grand Canyon

The Colorado River began carving the Grand Canyon approximately 6 million years ago. Some researchers believe parts of the canyon date back 70 million years. Today the Grand Canyon is so large and deep that it can be viewed from outer space. As the river carried away bits of the earth, it revealed many layers of exposed rocks. The Grand Canyon's walls are made of nearly 40 different rock layers. Most of the layers are sedimentary rock, but some are igneous and metamorphic rock. Geologists can learn about the area's past by looking at the changes between different layers.

How Sedimentary Rocks Form

As years pass and rain falls, more layers of sediment build up. The older layers are buried deeper. The top layers squeeze and pack down the bottom layers. In the course of tens of thousands of years, heat and pressure from within Earth slowly turn the bottom layers into rock. Over many years, sedimentary rock forms from layers of sediment.

The layers of rock that make up the Grand Canyon's walls in Arizona are nearly 1.8 billion years old.

These layers can sometimes be seen where a hill has been cut away to make room for a road. Canyons also show layers of sediment. Many different sizes of sediment can turn into rocks. Sediment can be as big as a boulder or as small as a speck of dust. Whatever the size, the pieces can get squeezed together to form a new rock.

Igneous and Metamorphic Rocks

While sedimentary rocks are formed by layers of built-up sediment, other rocks are formed through different processes. All rocks are made of minerals, or solids that are made up of different elements. Igneous rocks form when melted minerals from deep in the earth cool and harden. Igneous rocks can form when lava is spewed from a volcano. They can also form deep under the ground, when liquid rock cools and becomes solid. Metamorphic rocks start out as sedimentary rocks, igneous rocks, or other metamorphic rocks. These rocks are transformed into new rocks by extreme heat or pressure. The heat or pressure usually comes from deep in the earth.

The Rock Cycle

Earth's rocks are continuously formed, destroyed, and recycled

Uluru

Uluru is a huge rock rising out of central Australia. Also called Ayers Rock, this massive sandstone wins the award for Earth's largest chunk of rock. It rises 1,131 feet (345 m) above the ground, but that is only the tip of Uluru. More of the rock is buried under the ground. Like all sedimentary rock, Uluru has layers. At one time the layers were horizontal, but as time went on, Earth's movement caused the layers to tilt. Now they are vertical.

Uluru, a sedimentary rock in Australia, is the largest rock on Earth.

into something new. The recycled rocks are made of the same material as the old ones, but they have been changed into new rocks. This ongoing recycling is called the rock cycle. First, a volcano erupts. Hot lava pours out of the ground or slowly cools underground. As it cools, it hardens into igneous rock. Even rock that forms underground can eventually reach the surface after erosion. As time passes, rain falls on the rock and dissolves some of the minerals. Rainwater trickles into cracks and freezes, pushing outward and

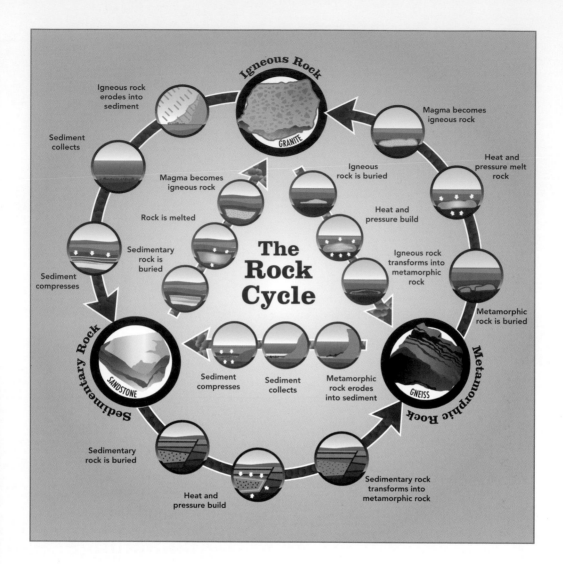

The Rock Cycle

splitting the rock. Plants begin to grow. Roots dig into the cracks and split the rocks even more. The rock breaks into smaller pieces. These changes are called weathering. Over time, the weathered bits wash away and turn into sedimentary rocks.

Later, the sedimentary rock may be squeezed or heated and transformed into metamorphic rock. In the rock cycle, any rock can be changed into any other kind of rock. Igneous, metamorphic, and sedimentary rock can all turn into metamorphic rock. All three kinds can be broken apart and cemented into sedimentary rock. And they can all be swallowed back into the earth, melted deep underground, and erupted from a volcano, turning into igneous rock again.

EXPLORE ONLINE

Chapter One focuses on how sedimentary rocks are formed and introduces igneous and metamorphic rocks. The website below also explains the three types of rocks. As you know, every source is different. How is the information given in the website different from the information in this chapter? What information is the same? How do the two sources present information differently? What can you learn from this website?

Rocks
www.mycorelibrary.com/sedimentary-rocks

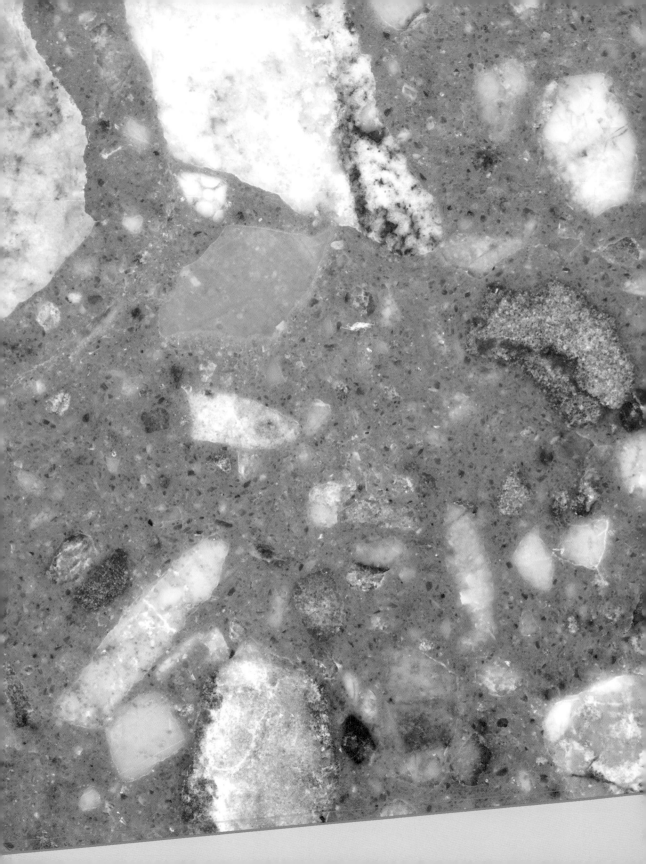

CHAPTER TWO

TYPES OF SEDIMENTARY ROCKS

Sedimentary rocks make up almost 75 percent of all rocks on Earth. They can be made of minerals, such as salt. They can also be made from the remains of living things pressed together. But most sedimentary rock is made of bits of other rocks. It can be made of sand, whole pebbles, or pieces of rock. The pieces can be large or tiny and rounded or jagged. Sedimentary rocks that contain pieces of

Breccia is a type of clastic sedimentary rock with coarse, jagged grains.

other types of rocks are called clastic sedimentary rocks. *Clastic* comes from a Greek word meaning "broken."

Clues in Rocks

Geologists study rock pieces, or grains, to learn about how a clastic rock formed. One clue is the color. Some grains are reddish-brown—the color of rusted metal. Rusted grains are a clue that the grains were once exposed to air and water. Another clue is the shape of the grains. Most pieces of rock start out with sharp edges and corners. Rocks worn by wind remain rough with sharp edges. Rounded grains are a clue that the pieces tumbled in a stream or river before they were cemented together.

Another clue is grain size. The size of a rock's grains can reveal what moved the pieces before they were cemented together. It takes glaciers, or massive rivers of ice, to move boulders, which are the largest rocks. Cobbles, which are smaller than boulders, are carried along by something not quite as strong. For

Rocks that spend time in rivers or streams become smooth and rounded.

SEDIMENTARY ROCK GRAIN SIZES

BOULDER
10 inches
(25 cm)
across or larger

COBBLE
2.5 to 10 inches
(6 cm to 25 cm)
across

PEBBLE
0.16 to 2.36 inches
(4 mm to 60 mm)
across

SAND
up to 0.08 inches
(2 mm)
across

SILT
too small
to see with
the naked eye

CLAY
too small
to see with
the naked eye

Grain Sizes

This diagram shows the different sizes of grains that can be pressed into sedimentary rock. Look at the pictures and think about how rock pieces can be moved from place to place. Which grains do you think move the most? What does their size, shape, and texture tell you about how much they move? Write 100 words describing the different ways that different-sized pieces can be moved.

example, quickly moving rivers or even landslides can move cobbles. Pebbles are so small they tumble along seashores or in rivers or streams.

Sand grains can be moved in many ways. They can be found in a river, in a mountain lake, or on the ocean floor. The smallest grains, which are clay and silt, are too small to see without a microscope. They are very light, and they float in quickly moving water. They settle to the bottom of quiet lakes, swamps, and rivers where the current is not strong.

Rocks from Living Things

Some sedimentary rocks are made from the remains of plants or animals. Limestone is a sedimentary rock that forms in warm, shallow seas where coral and animals with shells live. When these animals die, their shells and skeletons settle to the bottom. Over time, the layers build up. The pressure squeezes the layers into limestone. Limestone can be found in everything from cement to paint. It is even added to breakfast cereals to boost levels of calcium.

Coal is another form of sedimentary rock. It is made of dead swamp plants. When the plants die and drop into the swamp, they do not decay. The layers of

Coal, a nonrenewable resource from inside Earth, is widely used to produce electricity.

plants build up. Over thousands of years, they turn to stone.

Coal has many uses. Its main use is making electricity. The coal is taken out of the ground, trucked to a power plant, crushed, and burned.

The heat produces steam, which turns a generator to make electricity and power factories.

Oil is also used for energy. Oil is not a rock, but it is also formed from the hardened, calcified remains of very small plants that once lived in the ocean. Oil is used for heating homes and powering cars.

Oil

Oil is used to power cars and heat homes. But it has many other uses. It can be made into plastic bottles, car tires, compact discs, clothes, sneakers, and laundry detergent. It can be used to make preservatives in food. It can even be used to make medicine. Medicine was one of the first uses of oil thousands of years ago.

Coal and oil are fossil fuels. They were formed hundreds of millions of years ago. Fossil fuels contain the trapped energy of living things. They can be burned for energy, but they are nonrenewable resources. They cannot be replaced and will eventually run out with the rate at which humans are using them.

Rocks from Chemicals

Have you ever stirred sugar into a cup of tea? The tea tastes sweet because the sugar dissolves in the liquid. We call that a solution. Sometimes the dissolved minerals escape and become solid again. You have seen this if you have ever noticed grains of sugar at the bottom of a cup of tea.

Sedimentary rocks can be formed from solutions. The sugar at the bottom of the cup is a clue about how this happens. The dissolved mineral becomes solid and settles to the bottom in layers. Over time, it turns to rock. You won't find pebbles or sand in these rocks. Instead, these rocks feel powdery. Certain kinds of limestone form in warm seas that have calcium or magnesium dissolved in the water. The minerals become solid and fall to the bottom. The layers build up and are turned into limestone.

Gypsum is a mineral found in seawater. It settles to the bottom of sea floors. When seawater evaporates, it leaves a soft, white material behind.

Gypsum, a mineral that is left behind after salty seawater evaporates, can often be found in caves.

Salt Flats

The floor of Death Valley, California, is made of layers of salt and sedimentary rock. Death Valley is the hottest place on Earth. Here the ground is covered with a thick crust of salt over a large part of the park. The salt flat forms when rain falls in the nearby mountains. As the water rushes downhill, salt from the rocks dissolves in the flowing water. Soon the flat valley is covered by a thin layer of salty water. When Death Valley's heat causes the water to evaporate, salt crystals are left behind.

You can find gypsum in the walls of many homes. Very fine gypsum is called alabaster and is used to make sculptures. Another rock that forms through evaporation is rock salt. It forms when water evaporates from salty lakes, leaving the salt behind. In some places on Earth, there are layers of rock salt that are thousands of feet deep.

Could Mars have once had flowing water on its surface, just like Earth? NASA's Mars rover *Curiosity* has found areas on Mars where gravel and pebbles are worn down, similar to rocks in riverbeds on Earth. Scientist Asmus Koefoed believes worn rocks on Mars could prove water once flowed there:

> *Altogether we made a thorough analysis of 515 pebbles. . . . We could see that almost all of the 515 pebbles we analyzed were worn flat, smooth and round. We have classified them according to their geometry, which can be described using a single number . . . where 0 describes rocks that are completely flat like a piece of paper and 1 means they are perfect spheres. . . . In order to have moved and formed these rounded pebbles, there must have been flowing water.*

> Source: Asmus Koefoed. "Rounded Stones on Mars Evidence of Flowing Water." ScienceDaily. *ScienceDaily*, May 30, 2013. Web. Accessed December 18, 2013.

What's the Big Idea?

Take a close look at this quote. What is Koefoed's main point about these rocks? Pick out two details he uses to make this point. What does this information reveal about Mars's past?

CHAPTER THREE

CAVES

There are approximately 17,000 caves in the United States. Many caves begin forming in holes of sedimentary rocks. They form when the rock dissolves in water. Rocks made of salt and gypsum can form caves. Other caves are formed from limestone. Limestone caves are formed by rainwater, which picks up carbon dioxide from the air. Carbon dioxide is the same gas that forms bubbles in soft

Many caves around the world, including Wonder Cave in San Marcos, Texas, are tourist sites.

Lascaux Cave Paintings

In 1940 in France, four teenagers made an amazing discovery. As they followed their dog down a narrow entrance into a limestone cave, they stumbled upon a series of prehistoric cave paintings dating back roughly 17,000 years. Nearly 2,000 figures are painted or drawn on the walls of Lascaux Cave. Many are animals, including horses, cattle, and bison. This tells us that the people who painted them were hunters. The paintings weren't decorations in a prehistoric home. They are located too deep in the cave. Whoever made them had to crawl through a maze of dark tunnels to reach them. Why they were made is a mystery.

drinks. Water combined with carbon dioxide makes an acid. The acid is weak, but it is strong enough to dissolve limestone.

Most caves form in limestone. Every time rain falls, some of the water soaks into the ground. As the water trickles through the soil, it picks up more carbon dioxide. When the water bubbles down to the limestone underground, a little bit of the rock dissolves.

Flowing groundwater, or water within the earth, dissolves more of the rock. The dissolved limestone is washed away in streams and carried to the ocean. Slowly, holes are created in the limestone. Each time it rains, the holes get a little bigger. Over very long periods of time, a cave is created from these holes.

Sinkholes

Sinkholes can leave shallow bowl-shaped dents in the ground. Rainwater pools in these and funnels into the ground. When sinkholes or caves form underground, at first the ground stays intact. But if the holes grow large enough, the ground above can collapse, leaving a sinkhole in the ground. Sometimes the ground sinks slowly. Other times, it collapses suddenly, creating a hole in the ground. Sinkholes can be small or very large. A large sinkhole in Papua New Guinea is 1,148 feet (350 m) in diameter.

Cave Formations

While water can create dangerous sinkholes, it can also create wonderful features inside caves. These

In Lebanon, the Baatara gorge waterfall plunges into a sinkhole that is 837 feet (255 m) deep.

features make a cave look magical. Stalactites hang from the ceiling like icicles. The stalactite grows, drip by drip, as water seeps through cracks in the ceiling. The water contains calcite, a mineral from limestone. Before each drip falls, it hangs at the tip of the stalactite. A little of the dissolved calcite escapes and stays behind.

Stalagmites grow upward from the floor of the cave. As water drips from stalactites, it falls on the floor of the cave and splatters. The water evaporates, and the calcite is left behind. If enough time passes, a stalactite and stalagmite can join, forming a column.

Snottites

Stalactites and stalagmites are not the only things you'll find in a cave. Some caves have gooey structures called snottites. This slime coats cave walls. It can also drip from the ceilings of caves. What is behind these mucus-like cave formations? Snottites are made by bacteria, which are organisms too tiny to see without a microscope. Bacteria make the slime and live in it. That means snottites are not only gross, but they are also alive.

The Temple of the Sun room in Carlsbad Caverns National Park of New Mexico features both stalactites and stalagmites.

Over thousands of years, caves can turn into cave systems. The world's longest known cave system is Mammoth Caves in Kentucky. Four hundred miles (644 km) of caves have been mapped in this maze of connected caves. More caves have yet to be discovered.

Sinkholes can form suddenly, causing a lot of damage. This 2013 newspaper article describes a famous Florida sinkhole that captured the world's attention in May 1981:

> Barks from her dog Muffin first alerted resident Mae Rose Owens to a rapidly widening gap in her yard, and within hours a decades-old sycamore tree had disappeared into the void roots-first with what she later described as a "ploop" sound. . . . Her family did not evacuate until the following day, shortly before the hole opened further and took with it her three-bedroom house. Eventually the sinkhole grew to a width of 350 feet [107 m] and a depth of 75 feet [23 m]. . . . It took with it a car dealership and five Porsches, parts of two separate streets and the town's Olympic-sized swimming pool.
>
> Source: Richard Luscombe. "Florida's Most Famous Sinkhole." Guardian. Guardian News and Media, August 14, 2013. Web. Accessed December 19, 2013.

Consider Your Audience

Review this passage closely. Consider how you would adapt it for a different audience, such as your parents, your principal, or your younger friends. Write a blog post conveying this same information for the new audience. How does your new approach differ from the original text and why?

CHAPTER FOUR

SEDIMENTARY CLUES

Geologists study sedimentary rock in caves to learn more about caves and their rock formations. They can also study rocks to learn more about Earth's history. Clues to the past can be found in sedimentary rocks. When studying Earth's history, geologists use a geologic time scale. In this calendar, time is measured in millions and billions of

Geologists study layers of sedimentary rocks to uncover clues about Earth's history.

years. Understanding Earth's history requires a lot of detective work.

History in Rock Layers

Sedimentary rocks pile up. The older rocks are on the bottom. Newer rocks are on top. By looking at the order of layers, geologists can place rocks in the correct chronological order. The layers do not tell how long ago the rocks were formed, but they do show the order in which they formed.

Rock layers start out flat, but over time they can become folded or tilted. These changes can

Nicholas Steno

Nicholas Steno, a Danish scientist and priest, studied rock layers in the cliffs and hills of Italy. In 1669 he described the order of rock layers with a simple rule. He was the first to say that the youngest layers are on top and the oldest layers are on the bottom. Steno also realized that rock layers are flat at first. Layers that are folded or tilted were moved after they were formed. Steno even realized that fossils in different rock layers were like snapshots of history. They show different animals and plants living on Earth at different times.

Mountains form when the plates that make up Earth's crust push together and fold on top of one another.

be caused by large forces in the earth. How do these changes happen? The surface of the earth is made of enormous, jagged pieces called plates. The plates carry the oceans and continents on them. The plates move very slowly. Sometimes they squeeze together and form mountains. This is when rock layers become folded or tilted. The plates may also move apart from or slide past each other.

Fossils

As sediment settles on the lake or sea bottom, it may bury dead animals and plants. Time passes and the sediment is turned to rock. The animal and plant remains can become fossils. Fossils may be teeth, bones, or shells. They may be entire animals, animal skeletons, or plants. Most fossils are not the actual remains of the organism. They are the living things turned to stone.

When an animal dies, its soft parts quickly decay. Its bones decay much more slowly. As the bones slowly decay, they become filled with holes, like a sponge. Mineral-rich water can soak into the holes. As water continues to soak into the bone, the minerals build up. Over time, the original bone is replaced with minerals. In the end, the fossil has the shape of a bone, but it is made of rock.

A fossil can also be a mold of a living thing. This can happen when an animal leaves a footprint in mud. When the mud is turned to stone, the tracks

Some fossils are the remains or traces of prehistoric life, such as this pterodactyl.

are preserved. These fossils—called trace fossils—are often found in sedimentary rocks. Older fossils are found in older layers of rock. Newer fossils are found in newer rock.

Mary Anning

One of the most famous fossil hunters was a poor, uneducated woman. Mary Anning was born in 1799 in the town of Lyme Regis, England. She learned about fossil hunting from her parents. When Mary was 10 to 12 years old, she and her brother Joseph found a fossil of *Ichthyosaurus*, an ancient marine reptile. Mary discovered many more fossils. She became famous for her finds. Scientists came to ask questions about her finds. Her fossils helped change the way people understood the world.

Fossils are almost never found in igneous or metamorphic rocks. Why? You need a soft, mud-like material, such as layers of sediment, to make an imprint. When igneous rocks are soft, they are very hot. The heat burns up the remains of living things. Metamorphic rocks are made by intense heat and pressure. The heat and pressure destroy the remains that would become fossils.

The Fossil Record

All of the fossils that exist—both discovered and undiscovered—are called the fossil record. This record gives us a glimpse of past life on Earth. Only a tiny fraction of past life has been preserved as fossils. Animal remains must be buried quickly, and that doesn't happen often. For this reason, the fossil record does not show everything about Earth's history.

In addition, not all animals leave fossils. Hard-bodied animals are more likely to leave fossils. But soft-bodied animals decompose quickly. Fossils of jellyfish, worms, and insects are much less common than fossils of teeth, bones, and shells.

Reading the Fossil Record

Fossils and sedimentary rocks together tell a story. The deeper you dig, the further back in time you can see. The fossils change according to what lived on Earth at that time.

If you could look through the layers of rock in a steep cliff, what would you see? The bottom

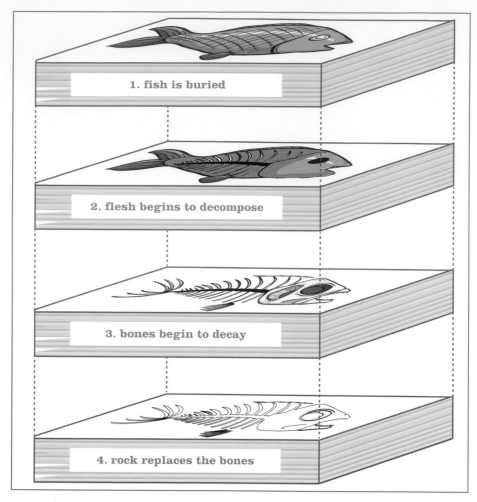

Fossilization

This diagram shows how an animal, such as a fish, is fossilized into rock. How does the information in the diagram compare to what you learned about fossils in the text? How does seeing the diagram help you better understand fossilization?

rocks and fossils are very ancient. The animals there

look different than the ones we know today. As you

move higher in the layers, you begin to see fish,

then amphibians, and then reptiles. Keep moving higher, and you will find dinosaurs. Finally, near the surface, you will find fossils of birds and mammals. Sedimentary rocks and fossils give us a picture of life over time. Together they show the many changes that have happened in Earth's history.

FURTHER EVIDENCE

There is quite a bit of information about how the history of Earth can be read in sedimentary rocks in Chapter Four. But if you could pick out the main point of the chapter, what would it be? Visit the website below to learn more about fossils. Choose a quote from the website that relates to Chapter Four. Does the quote support the author's main point? Or does it make a new point? Write a few sentences explaining how the quote you found relates to Chapter Four.

Fossils
www.mycorelibrary.com/sedimentary-rocks

Make Your Own Fossils

Press one inch (2.5 cm) of moist sand into a pan. Coat some small objects with petroleum jelly and lay them on top. In a separate bowl, mix equal amounts of sand and plaster. Add water to form a moist paste. Press a layer of this paste over the objects. Let the layers dry, creating a substance similar to sedimentary rock. When your "rock" is hard, turn the pan over and push it out. Brush away the sand to find your fossils.

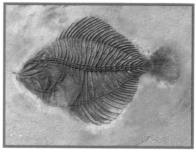

Dead plants and animals are often carried along with sediment in water, explaining why they are found in sedimentary rock.

Sedimentary Sandwich

Put a cracker, graham cracker, or piece of bread on a plate. Spread some peanut butter or cream cheese on top. Add whatever you like for the next layer, such as raisins, banana slices, brown sugar, honey, jelly, or grated coconut. Add the top cracker or piece of bread. How is your sandwich like layers of sedimentary rock? Which layers were "formed" first? Which were added last? Now munch away on your rock layers. Yum!

The layers of rock in the Grand Canyon reach depths of one mile (1.6 km).

Stalactites are formations of built-up calcite, a mineral found in limestone caves.

Salt Stalactites

Stir Epsom salt into three cups (0.7 L) of warm water. Keep adding salt until no more will dissolve. Pour the salt solution into two empty glass jars. Space the jars about one foot (30 cm) apart on aluminum foil or a baking sheet. Drape a piece of yarn or string between the two jars. Each end of the string should dip into the salt solution. In a few days, a stalactite will form on the string.

Take a Stand

This book discusses the fossil record. Do you think the fossil record gives us an accurate picture of the history of life on Earth? Or are there problems with using fossils to study Earth's history? Write a short essay explaining your opinion. Make sure to give reasons for your opinion and facts and details that support those reasons.

Tell the Tale

Chapter Three of this book discusses caves and cave features. Write 200 words that tell the story of your journey into a cave. Describe the sights and sounds that you might experience. What features do you see? What dangers might you encounter? Be sure to set the scene, develop a sequence of events, and write a conclusion.

You Are There

This book describes how teenagers discovered the cave paintings in Lascaux Cave in France. Imagine that you are one of the discoverers. How do you feel about your discovery? Do you tell someone about what you have found?

Say What?

Studying sedimentary rocks can mean learning a lot of new vocabulary. Find five words in this book that you have never seen or heard before. Use a dictionary to find out what they mean. Then write the meanings in your own words, and use each word in a new sentence.

GLOSSARY

acid
a compound that usually dissolves in water and reacts with a base to form a salt

decompose
to be destroyed or broken down slowly by natural processes and chemicals

erosion
the action or process of being worn away by water, wind, or glacial ice

geologist
a scientist who studies rocks and soil to learn about Earth's history

mineral
a solid chemical element or compound that occurs naturally from nonliving matter

salt flat
a hardened layer of salt on Earth's surface

sinkhole
a hollow place underground where drainage collects

solution
a liquid in which something has been dissolved

stalactite
a deposit of calcium carbonate resembling an icicle hanging from the roof or side of a cave

stalagmite
a deposit of calcium carbonate like an inverted stalactite formed on the floor of a cave by drops of water

LEARN MORE

Books

Brown, Cynthia Light, and Nick Brown. *Explore Rocks and Minerals!* White River Junction, VT: Nomad, 2010.

Dayton, Connor. *Earth.* New York: Windmill Books, 2015.

Hoffman, Steven M. *Rock Study: A Guide to Looking at Rocks.* New York: PowerKids Press, 2011.

Websites

To learn more about Rocks and Minerals, visit **booklinks.abdopublishing.com**. These links are routinely monitored and updated to provide the most current information available.

Visit **www.mycorelibrary.com** for free additional tools for teachers and students.

INDEX

ABOUT THE AUTHOR

Rebecca E. Hirsch is a former scientist and the author of dozens of books on science and nature. She lives in Pennsylvania with her husband, three children, one cat, and a small flock of chickens.